"STOP!"

How to control predatory chasing in dogs

David Ryan PG Dip (CABC), CCAB

ISBN 978-1-4092-5827-8

"STOP!"

How to control predatory chasing in dogs

David Ryan PG Dip (CABC) CCAB

Contents

Introduction

As a police dog handler and instructor I became fascinated by why and what dogs chased. Of course police dogs are supposed to chase, it's how they catch the bad guys, but they do it in a particularly controlled way and only on command. The chase could be in spectacularly difficult circumstances, perhaps over a series of gardens, hurdling hedges and scrambling fences, quite often in the dark and from the back of a van that had just screeched to a halt. The "prey" (and you'll see why I use that word later) was often more than twice the size of the dog and could be confrontational in the extreme when cornered.

To make sure that the dog would not let their handler, and the public, down by failing to catch the bad guys, we had to build up the desire to chase to extremely high levels. After all, what use is a police dog that won't chase in the dark, or across uneven ground, or if the prey looks too big? Dogs were selected, and later specially bred, for their high predatory chase instincts, and then that instinct was honed through training until they would chase anyone, anywhere, anytime. And they loved it. It would get to the stage where they weren't so much *commanded* to chase, just *released*.

Unfortunately for the handlers, and particularly the trainers, we were the good guys. We couldn't just cry, "Havoc!" and let slip the dogs, we were held to account for every mistake, so we couldn't afford to make any. Our dogs had to be under perfect control. If the bad guy had an attack of conscience as the dog was hot on his heels (and it is surprising how many were reformed by thirty-five kilos of dog fronted by forty-two glistening teeth coming at them at over twenty miles an hour), we weren't allowed to let the dog continue their planned trajectory. "Minimum force" was the phrase bandied about by the lawyers. That meant our dogs had to break off the chase on command too, no matter how close they were to achieving their original objective of firmly grabbing his right arm, spinning him round and knocking him to the floor. For those of you of a less than liberal disposition, who may believe that the bad guys deserve all they get, total control also provided a failsafe for when the proverbial small child stepped in front of us at the wrong time.

Not only had our dogs to be encouraged to chase until they were desperate enough to do it in any circumstances, they also had to be stopped from doing exactly that, sometimes right at the last moment!

Police dog trainers, me included, went through a variety of methods of increasing the drive to chase and an even bigger variety of ways of trying to control that chase drive. You could tell quite quickly during the selection process if the dog wasn't going to chase and it was easy to decide that they would never make a police dog. Sometimes teasing and frustration could help to awaken their suppressed desire to its full potential. But controlling the chase drive? Wow! Back in the dark ages of police dog training other instructors tried everything: giving food treats for the recall; increasing obedience commands to try to ensure compliance; tying them on a long line and giving the, "Stop!" command just before they reached the end; yelling at them louder and louder; throwing check-chains in front of them immediately after the, "Stop" command; strategically placing helpers to shout at the dog if they failed to comply; even up as far as using prong collars with sharp spikes to dig into the dog's neck and remote controlled electric collars to shock them into complying. These last two have long since been banned by police forces and armed services, but almost anything that doesn't actually hurt the dog still goes.

Some things worked for some dogs, but nothing worked for all dogs. The obedience based methods rarely worked when the dog was in high drive; the punishing methods reduced the drive to chase on command; the pain-inducing methods sometimes actually increased aggression towards the prey. We lived in an eternal conflict of finely balancing the drive to chase with the command not to and, like any fine line, we were often on one side or other of it. Too little drive and the dog was useless in a chase. Too little control and the dog was a dangerous liability. This is why many police dog trainers you will see have very little hair left.

But there were also other aspects of chasing that I observed police dogs performing. Some would chase rabbits or cats; some would chase sheep if they got the chance; most would chase a toy of some kind; I handled one that chased other dogs if he could!

The more I looked into dogs and chasing the more questions I raised. Why do they do it? Why don't they all do it? Why won't some stop? Why do some stop? Why chase some things but not others? What possesses a normally obedient dog to make them suddenly ignore you? What do you do if they don't stop? Why do they do it if they know it's wrong? Why are some prepared to absorb a lot of punishment to do it?

I only worked it out towards the end of my twenty-five year police dog training career, and then only with the benefit of a post graduate diploma from Southampton University. But once I'd put it together the light started to dawn.

Chasing prey is *normal* dog behaviour. Lots of dogs do it and some are bred to have no other function. Racing greyhounds and foxhounds for instance, and some of the more special police dogs. Once I'd worked out how to control it in police dogs, the challenge was to control it in pets. There are lots of books that tell you how to teach your pet manners, such as sitting and not jumping on the furniture, but those rules don't seem to apply when Fifi is off in hot pursuit of a squirrel.

What follows is the fullest explanation of canine predatory chase behaviour ever written. It answers all the questions, not just for police dogs, but for the misunderstood pets and the confused owners who can't stop them chasing. It also contains the most complete behaviour modification programme for avid chasers but, before we get to that, we need to get inside the canine psyche to understand what exactly predatory chasing is...

Chapter One
What Chasing Looks Like

There are lots of reasons why dogs decide to chase things and the whole range is beyond the scope of just one book so, in deciding what predatory chase is, it helps to look at what it isn't.

This list can't be exhaustive and some dogs will chase for a variety or combination of reasons, but let's have a look at some of the more common ones. These are some of the factors that can cause chasing and need to be ruled out:

- Social Agonistic.
- Fear.
- Territorial.
- Mating.
- Games.
- Somatic.

Social Agonistic chasing is probably the most common form, and it is basically part of a dispute. Contrary to popular belief, dog social behaviour, even arguing, is designed to minimise injury. With the dental equipment dogs have they could quickly dismember each other, and that would not be genetically sensible, so there is lots of posturing and bluffing. Chasing each other, either as a prelude to a more physical rough-house, or as part of an interaction where one breaks off and is pursued, is commonplace in dog society. In any disagreement there will be a victor and a vanquished but, on the way to deciding that, the more evenly matched may change roles frequently. The key pointers are that it will be towards another dog; it will usually not start until they are in close proximity; there will often be a history of dog to dog aggression and it will include scuffles of fighting.

Rushing towards another dog, possibly barking, probably with the front end high and the back end low, is not predatory but it's where the line blurs between social agonistic behaviour and fear. It seems strange to suggest that a dog might want to chase something of which it is afraid, but dogs only have three inherited strategies for dealing with things that frighten them: they can hide and hope it doesn't notice them, they can run away to put distance between them, or they can chase the scary thing away by being aggressive towards it. The key pointers towards fear chasing are that it will be a short chase because they will not actually try to catch the target; they will approach from the rear, and usually be content with driving it away with low back end, high front end, bared teeth, snarls and growls; if there is any contact it will probably be a quick bite and back off. Dogs will try to chase away things that scare them, particularly if they cannot get rid of the problem by hiding or running away, such as when they are on a lead or at home. However, chasing things away from their home is usually more often termed "territorial aggression".

Territorial behaviour could be regarded as a subset of fear. It is fear of losing access to an important resource: your home. Chasing what are perceived as intruders away usually starts as a normal fear response, with the accompanying fearful body language of low tail carriage, raised hackles and bow-wow-wowing bark but, as it becomes a successful way of driving away "intruders" such as the postman (every day he comes, is barked at, then leaves without entering) the dog becomes more confident in their ability to deal with the threat and as a result the body language also starts to become more confident. So it now doesn't look like fear and can actually be followed by head-on bites if the threat doesn't back down. It should only normally occur within defined boundaries, such as their home or garden, but also frequently happens from the car and sometimes in places where the dog is often walked, if they've decided it belongs to them.

On the other hand, chasing each other is also a doggy way of saying it with flowers. Mating would be a terrible thing if there wasn't any natural foreplay, and "chase me, chase me!" is the equivalent of a candlelit dinner for two, with wine. It will *usually* be between a dog and bitch and *usually* the bitch will be in or coming into season (although there are medical conditions that can make out-of-season females and male dogs attractive to other males) and, after a bit of playing hard-to-get, it will usually result in "a passionate embrace". Bitches that are not yet ready and dogs that have mistakenly attracted other dogs are likely to drop back into social agonistic behaviour, repelling potential boarders and it is definitely not a game.

Games are the practice of all the different types of reasons to chase and dogs will play fighting, defending and mating games. This may not just be with other dogs, but will usually happen with animals with which they are familiar, including humans. It doesn't usually happen with animals they do not know well enough. To play games you need to at least be introduced, if not good friends. It is easy for a game to boil over into the real thing, for example fighting games can become serious if one of the players bites too hard, so there is some overlap. Predatory games are no different to the real thing and will resemble it in every aspect, so other than a "game" is only played with friends and predatory chase can be towards a variety of targets, there *is* no difference.

To get a bit technical for a minute, play is regarded as being the non-functional display of adult motor patterns, either truncated or out of context. Which means that any predatory type behaviour that isn't actually intended to end in eating ("predatory" means hunting and killing for food) is really play. So all our police dogs are actually playing when they bring down a bad guy. Just don't tell the bad guys. Key indicators for "it's just a game" would be the frequent insertion of other behaviours into the predatory sequence, for example, rolling over, or changing roles with the other player. Dogs also use meta-signals like the play bow which indicate that they are only playing no matter how ferocious they look. However, obsessive predatory games played with a sibling may be as problematic as chasing next door's cat.

Somatic effects refer to medical conditions of the body rather than states of mind and there are a few, probably unmistakable, illnesses that can cause dogs to chase. Some types of tumour or forms of epilepsy can make dogs uncharacteristically aggressive and may involve chasing. Rabies can also involve a furious stage where dogs may run uncontrollably. Animals with these kinds of diseases may well appear manic, wild and angry. More importantly if your dog begins to exhibit any sudden onset of a new behaviour, or an unexpected increase in a previous behaviour, you should always get it checked out by a veterinary surgeon to rule out disease.

So, now we know what it *doesn't* look like, how do we recognise it? Well, if it is predatory chasing it will probably be exhibited towards more than one target: rabbits, cats, birds, joggers, cyclists, cars, livestock and sometimes, confusingly, even other dogs. The dog will seek out opportunities. Many dogs go missing in order to go looking for "prey". They will become excited by the smell, sight and sound of what they consider to be prey; quivering, yipping, and lunging on the lead. The chase could be preceded by searching or stalking, for example crouching in an almost cat-like pose. It can happen anywhere, although dogs will remember where they have performed it before and favour those locations. It can be stimulated by movement, for example it might only happen when the child, or the squirrel, starts to run. But most of all they actually look like they are enjoying it. They'll be flat out running, twisting and turning with the prey, open faced. Any noises they make will be happy ones, yipping in excitement or baying like a hound. Some dogs won't, or won't be able to, go for the bite, but those that do will probably grab at the rear end or back leg. If your dog does this, they have the predatory chase bug.

Chapter Two
Where It Comes From

So what is this decidedly stylised pattern of behaviours? Any predatory behaviour is part of the inherited predatory hunting sequence; a series of distinct motor patterns that canids inherit in order to prepare them to be able to learn how to catch prey to survive.

Wild, that is none-domestic, dogs couldn't possibly learn all the skills necessary to catch prey with each generation. It would be far too complicated to start from scratch with parents teaching pups every possible manoeuvre each time. Luckily they don't have to as they inherit the motor patterns; the actions necessary for each part. What do motor patterns look like? Err... how about some non-predatory ones as examples? Ones like "turning round several time before lying down" or "cocking his leg to pee" (you didn't think someone taught him did you?) or that strange thrusting motion he makes whilst gripping the vicar's leg with his front legs, or dropping his front legs to the ground and raising his bum in the air in a play-bow? All inherited motor patterns.

Motor patterns come into play when behaviours are complex, often in response to an emotional state, and it is likely that in wild dogs predatory behaviours are stimulated by hunger. It certainly makes sense that hungry dogs should start to search out prey, and that may be the very beginning of the predatory hunting sequence, a sequence that starts with travelling to a place where prey might be found and ends with eating that prey. In between those two extremes there are a number of possible actions that the dog might take. Consider this very basic series of hunting motor patterns:

- Tracking – the wild dog puts their nose to the floor and casts about for the scent of prey that passed by earlier. On finding such a scent they follow it.
- Searching – as they draw close to the prey, the wind carries the scent of the animal towards them, through the undergrowth. They lift their nose from the ground into the air to take advantage of the favourable wind directing them closer still.
- Seeing – they first clap eyes on their prey, and this is where alternatives may be deployed, depending upon what the prey does. Let's say it hasn't seen them yet, so there's no point in rushing at it whilst our hunting dog is still a long distance away.
- Stalking – getting closer to the prey can be done through lowering the profile and creeping closer with tiny movements. Inevitably there will come a point where the prey will be alerted to the dog's presence. Just before, or at that point, our dog will decide to make their play.
- Chasing – chasing too can be flexible. It can either be a mad all out breathless dash intended to catch the prey within seconds, or it can be a longer haul designed to wear down the prey over distance. Again, this may be determined by the prey itself. Is it fast? Is it old or young? Is it carrying an injury or parasite burden?
- Grab – the first bite may not be intended to dispatch the prey, but a grab to slow it down. There are different grabs to deal with different situations. If it is small prey coursed by a single dog, the grab might be at the back of the neck. Larger prey may be held by the hamstring or thigh muscle. Wolves working as

a pack may not all go for the same grab; some may target the hamstring, whilst others may grab for the animal's nose or throat. That's why it is difficult to say exactly which part our own chasing dog may go for.

- Kill-bite – this, as the name suggests, is intended to kill the prey. Often wild dogs preying on large game do not have a suitable kill-bite and the prey is worn down with many small bites. Small prey is often gripped firmly behind the head and shaken vigorously from side to side so that the neck or back breaks.
- Disruption – carcases need to be opened before our dog can feed and disrupting it is the process of taking the tough outer part away to expose the tastier innards.
- Feeding – finally our wild dog gets to actually eat by chomping and swallowing.

There are more predatory motor patterns involved in bird catching, mouse-pouncing, and digging, to consider just a few, but the above sequence gives us something to visualise when we eventually come to relate it to our pets.

To understand *how* it relates to our pets, we first have to consider how they differ from truly wild dogs, and the most obvious distinction is that our pets no longer have to hunt for their dinner. It comes in a tin of yummy meaty chunks, or a bag of vitamin enriched additive free organic munchies, dropped into their bowl at regular intervals. So why are they chasing things? Especially things they can't possibly eat, like bicycles, cars and aeroplanes! Well, feeding is only *part* of the predatory sequence and, like all the other distinct motor patterns, can become detached from it. To appreciate how that can happen we need to look at the process of domestication of the dog.

Dogs domesticated themselves about fifteen thousand years ago from the bolder wolves that hung about the rubbish heaps left by the newly settled humans. About that time some humans replaced the wandering hunting and gathering lifestyle with more permanent settlements. Where there are humans there are waste products, and waste products make a reasonable meal for a hungry wolf. Only certain temperaments of wolf were able to take advantage of this new ecological niche. The ones that weren't spooked so far or as often had the advantage of being able to eat more. As these wolves were changing into proto-dogs their inherited behaviours became less extreme because they no longer depended upon them to survive. Their brains, teeth and general body size became smaller because you don't need big teeth, brains or muscles to eat from the dump. The food arrives daily and you hang about in the meantime to conserve energy. Don't forget this was taking place over many hundreds of generations, so tiny inherited characteristics had time to develop to the advantage of the new dog-type dog. This was natural selection the way Darwin explained it. Tiny changes making the generations edge towards a better fit into their environment. Then artificial selection kicked in as well. From the human point of view there was no harm in having your rubbish eaten by scavengers who stayed just out of your range, and it could be handy to have a protein source relatively close for when the hunting didn't go too well, or the harvest didn't last through the winter.

Except you wouldn't want your livestock eaten or your children preyed upon, so any proto-dog that ate your chickens or chased people would be quickly killed or driven away. Now the genetic selection was for reduced expression of hunting behaviours. Only dogs with little or no inclination to hunt would be tolerated.

This is how the dog originated and still exists over the majority of the world. It is a smallish, inoffensive, scavenger of human waste, showing little if any hunting prowess. This is the basic dog; the one from which all our lovely modern breeds sprang forth. And boy, did they spring forth!

What we must remember is that, whilst our original scavenging dog did not exhibit hunting behaviours, it still held all the genes necessary for them. If every soldier carries a Field-Marshall's baton in their knapsack, every dog carries a wolf's genes within their chromosomes, they just don't use them all.

To cut a very long story as short as I can, there is slight genetic variation in every population. In every local group of interbreeding dogs, some will have slightly longer legs or shorter ears. In the same way, inherited behaviours will be subject to variation too. Some dogs will have more of an inherited desire to chase prey, or to search, track, stalk, or any other distinct motor pattern. People latched on to the idea that by breeding dogs that excelled at particular parts of the hunting sequence, they could increase their use.

The earliest evidence of dogs bred for a purpose are those of the ancient Egyptians, where dogs that look very similar to modern greyhounds were used for chasing antelope. But what good would they be if they chased it, caught it and ate it? Dogs that ate their catch were taken out of the gene pool, resulting in severing of the "kill" from the action of "eating" in the predatory sequence, probably at the point of "disruption" because that wasn't desirable either. You don't want your antelope carcase mutilated. This is still going on today. Hard-mouthed Spaniels that mutilate retrieved birds don't get to breed.

From there all kinds of specialist dogs were bred by increasing some parts and reducing other parts of the predatory hunting sequence. Dogs that tracked (bloodhounds, beagles); dogs that searched (setters and spaniels); seeing/stalking specialists (collies and pointers); even different grab-bites ("heeling" corgis and "heading" collies). We also have digging specialists and killing specialists in the terriers, sometimes both in the same dog.

That cute growl and shake of the fluffy toy is little Fifi's kill-bite, intended to snap the spine.

Every breed inherits the potential to develop increased parts of the original wild wolf/dog's predatory hunting sequence that defines their reason for being. Without increased "track" you're not a Beagle. Without increased "grab-bite", you're not a Lancashire Heeler. Of course, with the advent of the pet market increasing the breeding potential of even dogs that were rubbish at their original purpose, there are now lots of dogs that would fail to meet their parental aspirations as great hunters. The British Bulldog famously grabbed the nose of their prey, but some struggle to even breathe now. On the other hand, very few pet dog breeders consider the behaviour of their beautiful looking products.

What does all this mean?

It means that when you buy a puppy you can expect it to show at least some of the characteristics that the breed was originally used for. Expect spaniels to stick their nose on the floor and cast back and forth looking for scents. Expect Terriers to dig, Collies to herd, Labradors to pick things up. Some will hardly do it at all, some will do it to excess and the rest will be between the two extremes. Which brings us neatly back to chasing. Nearly all breeds of dogs, with the exception of some of the sheep guarding breeds, have the "chasing" part of the predatory hunting sequence in their breed make-up. It may be joined to other parts, or it may not, which is why not all dogs grab their prey and why some will catch it then stand looking a bit stupid, like they don't know what to do next. They haven't developed the next part of the sequence. If your dog is of mixed breed it can be really interesting to watch which breed specific behaviours develop. And dogs aren't currently being selected with behaviour in mind, unless you buy a working-bred puppy, when the breeders actually want enhanced "chase". So when you buy a puppy you get pot luck as to your pup's predatory behaviour, unless you specifically go for the working GTI version with double carburettors. Some people think they've bought a family runabout only to find that there is a Formula One engine under the bonnet.

Chapter Three
Developing Behavioural Conformation

But the racing car analogy isn't quite accurate. I need to rewind a bit. Technically, dogs don't actually inherit motor patterns in the form of fixed behaviour. They inherit the propensity to be able to develop certain motor patterns. They are born with the neural set up that makes the possibility of performing certain motor patterns more likely. Look at it like this: physical conformation is the shape of their body and behavioural conformation is the shape of their behaviour. When they are born they don't have their final body shape or their final behaviour shape. They have to develop both. In both cases, deprivation can stunt it and nourishment enhances it. In the case of behaviour, the performance of motor patterns will be switched on by coded genes at different times in a pup's development. If the pup doesn't get the opportunity to practice the motor pattern within the genetic window, it may never make the neural connections necessary for it to perform the behaviour later.

I mentioned earlier that sheep guarding dogs like Maremmas or Pyrenean Mountain dogs don't usually have "chase" in their behavioural make up. Any such dog that chased the sheep would not be suitable for the job. The method of training these flock guardians is to place them with sheep from the moment they can cope on their own. So much the better if mum is a worker, because they will be able to be around sheep before they are weaned. They therefore treat the sheep as their social equals. They never develop "chase" so they never want to chase the sheep. But because of the genetic variation in any population, some do develop it. Some go through a period where they start to chase things that move, at about six or eight weeks of age. And the only things there are sheep. Ooops! How do the shepherds control for that? They take the chasing puppy away from sheep for a few weeks and leave it in a shed until the desire to chase has passed. When the genetic window closes, the pup loses the desire to chase, their brain hasn't made the right neural connections and they never learn to perform the motor pattern of chasing. In some cases pups develop the chasing motor pattern by practising on other things and so don't direct it towards sheep. Remember that, it's important.

In a more domestic context, for example, most breeds (but some more than others, remember) have inherited the possibility to develop retrieving behaviour, but it needs to be grown in the brain. The exact onset/offset of the growing period hasn't yet been pinned down, but it is certainly whilst they are young. If pups are allowed to display retrieving behaviour within that window of possibility, the right connections grow in the brain. If they don't, the connections are never made and the behaviour doesn't develop. It probably isn't a well defined "critical period" but more likely a sensitive period that comes in slowly and recedes away gradually.

From experimenting with police dog puppies, we found that some would retrieve at six weeks and others wouldn't show any inclination until ten weeks, but practising once it kicked in certainly enhanced their future desire to perform it.

When the genetic window of opportunity opens, pet pups will actively seek out the chance to perform the behaviour.

At home the possibilities for chasing are endless, even at eight weeks: other puppies, cats, toys, ankles, children, the mop and anything else that moves. It is difficult to imagine a domestic environment that doesn't give a pup the opportunity to develop chase behaviour.

At this point we've determined that dogs, often randomly, inherit a propensity to develop a desire to chase and performance of that behaviour within a window of opportunity enhances its later expression. We don't know exactly when that window opens and closes, but it is certainly when they are still pups. So, from that we can conclude that if you're buying a pup, and you don't want them to develop a big chase drive:

1. Choose a non-chasing breed.
2. Make sure the parents aren't chasers anyway (Yes, I *do* know Pyreneans that have a chase problem).
3. Try not to enhance the part of the brain that will reinforce the behaviour in future by reducing the opportunities for chasing and increasing the opportunities for other puppy games.

That's okay when you have that kind of control over your future dog, but the reality is that many of us don't. We make mistakes by getting the "wrong" sort of dog, or choose one for looks rather than behaviour, or rescue an adult dog. If we need to change already fixed behaviour, that's always going to be more difficult.

Chapter Four
Why Dogs Chase

When we have a dog that is already chasing, we have to ask ourselves a question. That question isn't "How do I stop my dog chasing (joggers, sheep, cats, etc)?" or even, "Why does my dog chase (fill in blank)?" It is, "What does my dog get out of chasing?"

The answer is "dopamine". We've already established that such a dog must have had a genetic propensity to be able to build a brain that can reinforce the inherited motor pattern and that, as a pup, must have developed their brain through practice.

What such a dog gets out of performance of the motor pattern of "chase" is internal reinforcement through the neurochemical dopamine. Dopamine is the feel-good neurochemical that gives us all a buzz when we score that goal, ski down that hill, get that exam result The one that sends endorphins whizzing round our bodies; that makes us feel so alive, so exhilarated! It is also the same brain reward neurochemical that is abused by users of cocaine and ecstasy, so you can imagine the addictive qualities.

Dogs that chase are internally reinforced through just performing the behaviour. They do not need any form of external reinforcement, even through catching the prey, because the behaviour is reinforcing in itself. That last sentence is probably the most important one in this book, so I'm going to repeat the most significant bit. *The behaviour is reinforcing in itself.* Put simply, they enjoy it; hugely. They enjoy the high they get from it so much that they close down other senses to concentrate on it. As well as extraneous senses (smell, hearing, touch) being reduced, so is the capacity to feel pain. All focus is on the target as the source of pleasure. That is why dogs will run through barbed wire and thick brambles, being cut to shreds in the process, when they are chasing. That's why normally road-sensible dogs will run out in front of cars. That's why owners cannot recall their dogs when they are in full flight. Their dogs simply don't hear them.

Dogs with a high chase drive not only derive great pleasure from it, they also *need* to perform it. They are driven to perform the behaviour to receive the boost to their well-being it provides. They are constantly looking for outlets for their chase behaviour.

If an owner has a dog with chase drive inherited towards the top end of the continuum, they often find them difficult to control. The problem is that it is very difficult to counter internally reinforced behaviour with operant conditioning. Operant conditioning is the usual way we train dogs. It is a reward contingent upon the dog performing a behaviour that we want, for example, "Sit and I'll give you a pat", or "Come here and I'll give you a biscuit."

An example might help you to understand... Imagine I'm playing centre forward for England in the world cup final against Brazil. It's nil-nil with two minutes to go and once again I'm running at the best defence in the world. I see Steven Gerard cross over onto the right wing and I lob a perfectly weighted ball into his path, sprint into the penalty area and scream for the return. Wayne Rooney draws the right back out wide as Stevie G hammers the ball back beyond the first defender towards me at the far post and, as I rise to meet it, the Brazilian goalkeeper slips. I'm about to volley my way to a world cup winner's medal and into English footballing history when, faintly, I hear you yell from the touchline, "Stop that now and I'll give you a biscuit."

What do you think are the chances that I'll stop?

Think of the thing that you most enjoy. The thing that gives you the biggest buzz: squash, skiing, show jumping, sailing, extreme ironing... Would you give it up for a biscuit? No? Neither will your dog. A dog will not stop chasing for the promise of a biscuit simply because a biscuit is not as valuable as the internal dopamine boost from the chase behaviour. In fact, *nothing* is more valuable than the chase.

You'll find people who will say that they've trained dogs to come back from a chase with a biscuit, and I have, too. Dogs with lower chase drives *will* comply and dogs with higher drives may comply for a while, but if they are not given the opportunity to express their chase behaviour the drive to chase will eventually outweigh the value of the operant reinforcer (the biscuit).

This is the second reason owners cannot control dogs in full flight. They haven't got anything the dog wants more than what it is doing now.

If you try to punish a dog for chasing it might also work for a while, but positive punishment is just another form of operant conditioning where the dog is exposed to an aversive stimulus when it performs the unwanted behaviour.

It will break down eventually, or you will have to continue the punishment each time. We'll visit punishment again later, but suffice to say that, if you are able to punish the dog into stopping, without doing anything else, you never really had a chase problem.

The biggest problems with punishment come from the additional consequences, for example, from the dog's point of view:
"I know chasing sheep feels good.
I am beaten when I am caught chasing sheep.
The sheep chasing is the good bit.
The being caught is the bad bit.
Sheep good, people bad.
Chase sheep, avoid people."

Remember, the behaviour is only unwanted by us. It isn't a problem for the dog, because they were born to do this. It is normal behaviour for this particular animal and actually preventing them from chasing may well compromise their emotional welfare.

Dogs have a limited number of ways that they can regulate their emotions. Performing internally reinforcing behaviour is a way of increasing their store of good emotions to combat the challenges that they face on a daily basis.

We all do it in one way or another. A bad day at the office demands a large bar of chocolate, a beer, a hot bath, or a work-out at the gym. We raise our emotional state. Dogs don't do beer or bubble-baths, but they chase. If they can't chase, how else can they improve their miserable state?

These are examples of behaviours that can result from dogs denied the opportunity to chase: constant barking, flank sucking, chewing the walls and furniture, catching imaginary flies, indoor toileting, humping the cushions, howling when left, eating faeces, biting the kids, tail chasing, leaving home, licking legs and feet until they bleed, urinating in bed, digging up the garden, swallowing stones, stalking the TV, bouncing off the walls, crying all night, fighting with other dogs... and these are just some of the possibilities.

You can't just *stop* these dogs from chasing. You can't *persuade* these dogs not to chase for the promise of a biscuit. You can't *punish* these dogs to make them stop chasing. Depriving them of the opportunity to chase may well *compromise their welfare*. So what can we do? We appear to have a dilemma. These dogs *have* to chase, and it seems we have no means of stopping them because the behaviour is inherited and therefore internally reinforced. There isn't anything they would rather do.

All of that is true, but the light-bulb moment, the one where we realise that we actually know the answer to this, comes with the understanding that the behaviour is inherited, but the target of that behaviour is learned. Otherwise, how do we get spaniels to search for drugs, or German Shepherds to search for people? It's the drive to search that's inherited, not what they are searching for!

And if we can control the target of the behaviour, we can control the behaviour. Nothing is more valuable than the target, because the target is the access to exhibiting the behaviour. Access to scoring a goal is a better reward than a biscuit. But how do we control the target? It isn't possible for us to control the sheep, rabbits and cars, so we have to change the target to one we *can* control.

The problem arises because most dogs choose their own chase targets and it is quite likely that they will choose sheep, cats, rabbits, aeroplanes, joggers, cyclists, cars, birds... because they are the things available in the environment. Remember, they are actively seeking opportunities to chase. They then get stuck in a neural positive feedback loop, where the running rabbit stimulates the chase, the chase provides the buzz, and therefore rabbits are access to the buzz. They provide their own reinforcement for the behaviour of chasing rabbits, and behaviour that is reinforced is likely to be repeated.

Most dogs have their own hierarchy of preferences, dictated, amongst other things, by access to their range of targets. For example, if they've chased rabbits 100 times, sheep 50 times, cars 20 times and tennis balls 10 times, and all four appear in front of them at the same time, they will prefer to chase the rabbit. The other ones will do if there are no rabbits about, but the most chased target will be the preferred one. This is a bit of an over-simplification as targets have innate properties themselves, small furry things are more attractive to chase than stones for example, but you get the idea. Each dog will be different, so we'll never know the precise figures, but it is likely that to make a stone a preferred target over a rabbit you will have to make a lot more joins between "chase" and "stone" than "chase" and "rabbit" in the brain. The principle holds, however, and I do know a Staffordshire Bull Terrier that runs through a field of rabbits to get to the stones at the river. (Yes, I know it's not a good idea for a dog to chase stones!)

The secret to success in controlling chase behaviour therefore, is to control the target. We found that with police dog pups that hadn't developed preferences that was relatively easy and we focussed them on things that they were likely to be asked to find as part of an investigation, such as mobile phones, or car keys. With older dogs that had established preferences it takes slightly more time and effort. But it can be done.

When I started police dog handling most of the dogs were donated as one to two year olds by members of the public, but as the German Shepherd pet population became more suited to family life (have you noticed how much *nicer* GSDs are these days?), they became less suitable to train as police dogs. Too calm, not enough inherited chase drive. This forced the police into breeding their own strains of more driven dogs that are more suited to the role.

However, the specialist police dogs, the ones used for sniffing out drugs, explosives, cadavers and, more recently, blood spots, are often still taken as adults from the working strains of Labradors and Spaniels. If you have been paying attention, you will realise that working type behaviour can also sometimes surface in the pet population, too. The police still take pets that are going stir crazy through not being able to behave like they were working animals, from members of the public who are at *their* wits' end. It is the round peg and round hole situation. The dogs want to work and the police want workers. They also take failed gundogs, usually because they are too strong, which is shooting speak for, "Won't stop working when they are told". All of these dogs come with a huge inherited drive to chase, because it is what the police look for, but it is often directed towards birds, rabbits, sheep... you know the usual list.

Obviously the police don't want their dogs running off after rabbits whilst searching woods for a drug stash, or disappearing into the pond after a duck when clearing a route of bombs, so that chase behaviour has to be reoriented.

That is done by not allowing access to the previous target and focussing the chase onto a new one, usually a tennis ball or a Kong. Take them away from rabbits and play ball. And play ball, and play ball, and play ball. Until they are mad for the ball. Then play ball in a field where there *used* to be rabbits... Eventually the tennis ball becomes the preferred target, the *most* preferred target and the dog will do anything to gain access to it.

What most specialist police dogs work for is access to their chase target, although the soft old coppers call it their toy. They're not hooked on drugs, they're not fed food treats, and they're not obediently complying. They're allowed access to their chase target conditional on finding the substance for which they have been trained. And such is their addiction to *chasing* they will go through hell and high water to earn a throw.

The reorientation of a chase target isn't just training, it is a total change in behaviour. A Behaviour Modification Programme that will work for you, too. But because you are probably not a police dog handler (breathe a sigh of relief) we need to expand this BMP to fit all pets and all circumstances, so the remainder of this book is devoted to the most complete behaviour modification programme for the most difficult dog to control.

Chapter Five
The Foundations

Those of you who are not familiar with the concepts of behaviour modification as practiced by professional pet behaviour counsellors may not know that every behaviour modification programme is a compromise. In every case we will look at the problem and work out the perfect programme that has the maximum effect. In every case we then start to trim that perfect programme to fit the individual circumstances, which include the dog, the owner and the past and current environment.

As I don't have that information for you and your dog, what follows is the maximum intervention programme for the most difficult dog. Consequently the responsibility for trimming it falls to you. There will be a temptation to skip the earlier bits, the less sexy bits that don't yield immediate results but take time and effort. Don't. These are the most important parts to the overall result. Indeed, if you get some of the earlier sections right, you won't need the later ones, saving you time and effort in the long run. Miss out the earlier sections and the rest won't work anyway.

I've lost count of the dogs that have been presented to me with a chase problem that wouldn't come back even when they *weren't* chasing.

To train a dog to do, or not to do, anything is an incremental sequence of small steps. Sure, you will see trainers make short-cuts, huge leaps that have instant results, but without the basics this training will eventually break down and you'll be worse off than you were before. You can't reintroduce the dog at the point it failed, you have to go back to the beginning and start again, only this time the dog has some more learning experiences you will have to counter.

I also get the, "The only time he misbehaves is when he is chasing, so I don't need all the rest." answer. It doesn't matter whether your dog's other behaviour is *acceptable* or not, that you don't *need* them to lie down when you ask, what matters is that to control the chasing you both need to be versed in the basic exercises.

If this hasn't persuaded you to start at the beginning and redo until perfect, then perhaps I should tell you that implementing these earlier parts will immeasurably improve your dog's perception of you, and your relationship with them. If you're not convinced by now, you were probably always destined to fail anyway!

The good news is that because each dog is an individual, the programme can be left as soon as the behaviour is under control. You don't need to soldier on to the end if your dog doesn't warrant it. However, I can appreciate that determining exactly how much intervention is required may be difficult, so if in doubt, start right at the beginning and aim for the maximum. You can always pull out when the behaviour is resolved.

The start point is to stop the rot. Prevent all reinforcement of inappropriate chasing. We need to stop the current target continuing to be reinforced through constant repetition. To do that we have to remove the composite stimulus. It is not just the sight of the target that predicts its reinforcing properties. It is also the smell and sound.

If your dog's ears twitch before they adopt the crouching stalk, or they glue their nose to the ground, snuffling and moving back and forth, they are likely to be picking up on some part of the composite stimulus. I was working with an aeroplane chasing Border collie (we have a lot of low flying jets where I live) that used to pursue them to the horizon. Whilst dealing with it we always walked him on a long line, but we would know when one was approaching because he would go into the classic Border collie crouch on hearing it approach, long before we did. The sound was part of the composite stimulus that predicted the pleasure of the chase.

You must remove as much as possible associated with the inappropriate target or targets; all sight, sound and smell of them, and remove the dog from all areas associated with them. If you are really good at this you may also identify other parts of the composite stimulus, like particular clothing you wear to go particular places. Sit down and work out exactly what your dog associates with the targets, so that you can filter it out. As you will see later, this is not just an option, it is essential to success. With newly recruited police trainees we played inside buildings rather than risk competition with the old targets. Take them swimming, drive to the beach, play games in your back garden, do *anything* else, but prevent further reinforcement. Would it hurt just once in a while to take them to a rabbit field? Occasional reinforcement strengthens the response even more, and makes it resistant to extinction, so the occasional lapse will make it immeasurably more difficult to control. Yes, of course there is a reality check. If you really can't prevent access to the whole stimulus, minimise it the best you can and hope that your dog isn't as committed as you think they are.

That was an easy step. Nothing to do but stop doing things. The next step involves more thought. We need to increase their emotional bank balance. All of us need positive experiences to balance out the challenges to our emotional wellbeing. Too many challenges or too few positive emotions and we go into deficit. Because our bodies can't tolerate too much deficit in the form of stressors, we are driven to improve our emotional state by any means we can. Remember? Beer and chocolate? Or maybe you prefer massage, or meditation?

By stopping the rot, we are temporarily removing a major source of positive emotions for our chasing dog, perhaps the only one! Consequently their overall emotional contentment may plummet. This will cause them to seek out other occupations to try to give themselves a lift. Remember? Bark, Suck, Chew, Dump, Hump, Howl, Lick, Wet, Dig, Swallow, Stalk, Bounce, Cry?

We need to balance their emotions, but we can't do that before we have decided what they consider to be challenging. We need to do a scan for possible sources of anxiety in their environment and consider what we can do about them. Possibilities may include loneliness, noise, confrontation, individual family members, other pets, sources of punishment. The secret is predictability and control. If I can predict a source of stress I can find a way to deal with it. If I can control a source of stress, I can remove it. It may be as simple as giving the dog a bed where it can get out of the way of a visiting toddler, providing chews to eat when you go out, getting a dog walker to provide an extra walk, playing games with food balls or stuffed Kongs, or it may be as complicated as a major anxiety reduction programme requiring a change of diet and veterinary intervention. If it is the latter, you need specialist help from a behaviour counsellor to build that programme before you can start on the chasing problem. Details of the Association of Pet Behaviour Counsellors can be found at the end of the book.

Having done the scan and addressed as much as you can, we need to implement a strategy that has become a staple of behaviour counsellors recently. It is known variously as Learn to Earn, N.I.L.I.F (Nothing In Life Is Free), Holistic or Lifestyle Training.

It consists of taking control of the things dogs find most important. These resources are of major value in varying degrees to individual dogs but not necessarily to us. They are Food, Toys/ Games, and Attention and each dog will place different values on each one but, taken together, everything a dog values can be placed in one of the three categories. There is a fourth one, "Reproduction" but that is beyond the remit of this book. Basically, the dog must say, "Please" in order to earn access to anything in the three categories of resources.

Let's start with Food, because that's easiest to explain. As you would for a child, ask the dog to say "please" before they are given their food or any treats. Don't worry, we don't have to teach them to speak, we just ask for a deferential behaviour in order to earn access to the food. Training treats are fine, because they always do something for you to get one, but don't just place their food bowl on the floor and walk away. Stand in front of your dog with the bowl and say "sit" just once. If they don't know how to sit, raise the bowl above their head until their bum hits the floor and you can train them to sit at the same time. When they sit, lower the bowl to the floor. Most dogs will get up to approach the food. Simply say, "Ah" and pick up the food again. Do not repeat "sit", but wait until they sit again and lower the bowl to the floor. After a few false starts they will back off and not try to take the food. At that point say, "Okay" and let them eat. They earn the food by performing a deferential behaviour, by backing off. We have done it through controlling the resource (the food) rather than the dog. They voluntarily defer to us in order to get something they want and it helps with their understanding of communication. This applies to all food, even your left over toast crust but, if left to evolve with mealtimes, only gives us a couple of training opportunities each day. To speed up the process and teach them some better communication skills, we can train it as a separate exercise.

Take some treats in your left hand and place one in the open palm of your right hand, sitting facing your dog. Put your left hand behind your back as the treat reservoir, handy but out of the way.

A word about treats whilst we're using them. People say, "My dog isn't really into food treats". How can that be? Think about it. Food is a basic staple of life. People fight wars over food. Wild canines expend a huge amount of time and energy seeking out food. What people mean is that their dog isn't sufficiently interested in the treat in their hand. There could be two reasons for this. Firstly they may not be hungry. Counter that by training before meals, or missing a meal until after training. Secondly they may not be interested in the type of treat. Dried doggy kibble or bought-in treats don't always tug their rug. Try smelly cheese, left over crispy chicken skin, anything fishy, hot dog sausage or chopped dried liver. Find something your dog really likes. When you have, chop it into tiny bits, about pea-sized for big dogs and half that for littler ones. It should be gone in one gulp. The idea is to give just enough to tempt them with a flavour and so they immediately want some more. Only giving tiny pieces also allows us to train for longer, before they lose their hunger.

Back to communication-skills training. We're sitting facing our dog, palm extended with a delicious treat on it. At this point they will probably try to take the treat. Calmly close your hand and say "Ah". As soon as they back off, open your hand again. When they try to grab, say "Ah" and close it again. That is not good manners. If you want to sit with a piece of food on your hand, it does not give them the right to take it. It belongs to you. After several repetitions they will back away from your hand, slightly perplexed that their usual strategy of grabbing hasn't worked. Immediately say, "Okay" and offer the treat into their mouth. Replace the treat from the reservoir behind your back and start again. You are introducing two new communication words. "Ah" means, "Doing that won't work" and, "Okay" means, "That worked!" Soon they will be backing off in order to earn the treat from you. It is your treat and you can give it to them whenever you want. If you want them to have it as a reward for deferential behaviour rather than pushiness, then that is your prerogative. As they begin to understand, they will back off every time. This is the time to extend the deference by using feedback commands. These are the, "Good dog, clever dog," kind of words said in a pleasant voice that encourages them to keep doing what they are doing. They mean, "You are in the right area, keep doing that and eventually you will get a treat for it", and help to prolong behaviours. As you do this they will probably go through a series of other things that have previously won a reward, such as lying down, pawing, or play-bowing. What you are aiming for is eye contact. After failing to win the treat through different strategies, most dogs eventually look you right in the eye as if to say, "What do you want me to do?" That is the time to "Okay" and reward. Once you have rewarded eye contact once, they will give it sooner and more reliably. Using feedback commands, extend the eye contact until they look at you for up to thirty seconds. Use the same "Ah," "Okay" and feedback commands in all your training to maintain consistency and ease of understanding. You can use different words if you like, but make sure the family all agree which ones, so you all use the same communication.

Toys and games are the expression of the very chase drive we are trying to control and we are going to use them to change our dog's behaviour, so we need to understand how dogs relate to them. There are two types of toy for dogs: ones that they play with by themselves or with other dogs, Free Play Toys, and ones that we play with them, Interactive Toys.

It's a good idea to keep free play toys in a toy box, so that you have control over their use. Select toys to give to your dog when you wish, and put them away again when you want to. Rotate your dog's toys, a couple today, a different couple tomorrow. This increases the value of the toys and the amount of time they play with them, because they are not always available, and it increases *your* value, because you provide "new" toys every day.

When *you* play with toys with your dog, they also get your attention. A double whammy! The toy should come out when you want to play and go away when you are done. This gives your dog clear signals about playtime and gives the toy immense value. If you want to put an even clearer signal on playtime by giving them a "Playtime!" command and a "Finished" command, so much the better. We'll look at how and what to play later.

The third resource, "Attention", is perhaps the most difficult for people to get a handle on. We have dogs because we like to interact with them. What we mustn't forget is that our attention is ours to give when we want, not when we are manipulated into giving it by a puppy. This is not a "no attention" programme, in fact you can give as much attention as you like. What you need to be aware of is exactly when you give attention, and what your dog perceives they did to earn it. Attention is speech, eye contact, and touch. Remember, behaviour that is rewarded is likely to be repeated, and any kind of attention, even negative attention like being shouted at, is more rewarding than none at all. Dogs do what works for them. If you ignore calm relaxed behaviour but shriek and chase them when they pinch your socks, they'll keep pinching socks.

Give your dog lots of attention, but make it conditional on good behaviour. If your dog bites your knees and you jump up and down, it is likely to repeat the behaviour. If they are ignored when they sit quietly on the mat, they are less likely to repeat that behaviour.

If your dog pesters you for attention, actively ignore behaviour you don't like. Stand up, turn your back, fold your arms, do not speak and look away (because attention = speech, eye contact or touch). If it is really bad walk out of the room, but only until they stop or for five seconds at the most. Better still, don't wait until they've done something bad. You can almost always predict the times that bad behaviour will happen, so pre-empt it and give your dog an opportunity to do something you do like, instead. Tell them to fetch a soft toy and then reward with lots of fuss. Ask them to sit on a mat, or lie down, or any non-invasive behaviour, but *don't forget to reward them*. Behaviours that you like will become more frequent, and other behaviours will decrease.

A word of warning for the owners with the most persistent dogs: if you are retraining non-invasive behaviours at the expense of previous undesirable ones, it may get worse before it gets better. Your dog has always had a response before, and now doesn't get it, so may do their particular demanding behaviour more, or even try new behaviours through frustration. Stay calm, remember what you are aiming for and reward the nearest thing you can get to it. Even a momentary sit can be rewarded and built on later.

Other unrestrained behaviours can be brought under control in the same way. Uncontrolled behaviours such as doing the wall of death round the living room when you pick the lead up, or barging through doors ahead of you, are the dog's attempt to control access to games, in this case represented by going for a walk, and can be returned to your control by the same method. Take control of the resource rather than competing with your dog.

If they go loopy when you pick the lead up, put it down again and ask for a sit. Same as the food bowl, they don't get access to this important resource unless they defer by sitting quietly. Sure, it takes a while at first, but persistence will more than make up for a few false starts in the long run. If your dog barges past you through doors, teach them to wait until you allow them through. Bring them to the door and take hold of the handle. Ask for a "sit" then open the door a crack. If they move their bum at all, say, "Ah" and close the door again. When they sit, open the door a crack. If they remain sitting open it a crack further. Any movement results in the door closing, any deferential sitting results in it opening. When the door is fully open and your dog is still sitting quietly, say, "Okay" and allow them through. You don't have to go through first. Dog trainers that insist you go through first are missing the point, it isn't beating your dog through that raises your status, it's controlling access to the resource.

Why are we going to all this bother when it is the chase that we are trying to control? Well, a dog that pays you more attention generally will be easier to recall from a chase. A dog that checks in with eye contact for permission to access resources will think before setting off on a chase. A dog that knows you control games is going to be far more amenable to stopping inappropriate ones. A dog that waits to be invited through doors will be less likely to barge past your wishes when you stop them chasing.

Many owners ask for advice to stop their dog from chasing when they aren't under control at any other time. Learn to Earn is the basis for a relationship in which the dog voluntarily defers to us, but to build on that you also need basic obedience.

There are plenty of books and trainers for basic obedience, and most owners are capable of teaching their little treasure how to sit and maybe even lie down, so I'm not going into this in the same depth. The proviso is that you really do need to revisit your obedience training, because if your dog is chasing and you can't stop them, they aren't obedient enough. Essential points for training obedience are:

- Teach at least "sit", "down" & "recall" *for reward*.
- Use the maximum reinforcer – very tasty treats or exciting games.
- Incorporate communication skills.
- Teach holding eye contact in different places.
- Start in a place with no distractions before introducing them gradually.
- Aim for ten out of ten sits in the park on first command.

Only then can we start to put the meat on the bones of this programme by progressing to the retrieve. Before we do that, we need to say goodbye to those owners whose dogs have just stopped chasing. The ones who needed some sources of anxiety removing, a bit of emotional stability and firmer rules in order to stop when asked. There'll be quite a few dogs whose lives are now so improved that they don't need to chase any more.

The rest of us, who have now made our dogs' environment as stress free as we can, have stabilised their emotions by taking control and improved their obedience, but still can't stop them, need to take the next step.

Chapter Six
Retrieve, Retrieve, Retrieve

By, "Retrieve" I mean "Go and collect the toy every time when asked and bring it back all the way to me, not stopping on the way, then give it up voluntarily". So if you think your dog retrieves by picking the toy up and running around with it in their mouth, think again. In fact, don't just think again, but train it again! Like all dog training you should start in a place with no distractions. Lock the doors, close the blinds, put the light on, switch the telly off, take the phone off the hook, tell the neighbours not to come round, send the kids out to play and just teach your dog. When they are proficient in those circumstances, introduce distractions gradually by playing in the back garden, where it is quiet, then the front garden with passers-by passing by, then in the park, but at quiet times when no one else is about. You get the picture? Always expect regression when you introduce new distractions into training, but persevere and it will build up to previous levels again.

Like any other training, short bouts and lots of them yield the best results. In police dog training there are usually six dogs in a class. Each one has a go, and then takes a break to allow the others their turn. By the time they come around again they are refreshed and keen to give it another try.

This is best practice for any kind of dog training but, like any kind of dog training there will be those that it won't work for. The biggest problem you are likely to encounter with prey chasing dogs is that some are so turned on to their original target that they won't even look at anything else. Okay, time to get inventive. The emphasis now is on simulating the behaviour of the problem target, with one massive condition. Never make the new target appear to be the old target. It may be very tempting to stuff a rabbit skin with rags, but how is that changing the target? What matters is what is in your dog's mind. If they think they are chasing a rabbit, it strengthens that response and we are making matters worse. Make the new toy *behave* like the old problem target, but not resemble it too closely.

This stimulates the dog to chase but, when they catch it, they are reinforced by something new. If they chase and catch what they believe to be a rabbit it strengthens the desire to continue chasing rabbits. But they may be so tuned in to rabbits that they are only turned on by the properties of a running rabbit. So we may have to excite by simulating running rabbit behaviour, but they should catch something that is definitely NOT a rabbit.

Choose targets to suit the individual dog and their preferred behaviour: for sheep chasers use big footballs or boomer balls, for bird chasers try Frisbee, for rabbit chasers use Kong rolled through leaves, for "killers" try a ragger. Not interested? Try a gravy soaked tennis ball or sock on string, a shuttlecock, biscuits, stuffed Kongs or one of the vast array of commercially produced toys on the market.

Consider smell, taste, texture, chewability and the behaviour of the toy. If you *have* to use a squeaky or furry, change a significant aspect of it, for example, make it smell or taste strongly of something else. Aniseed? Cheese? Vanilla? Fish? Liver? When caught, the properties of the *new* target reinforce the chase behaviour.

Make the target move like prey, jerky and unpredictable along the ground or flying. Balls can be rolled past, bounced alongside or tossed over, depending on the dog's preference. Use excitement and consider social group facilitation. Play between yourselves or with another dog to see if your dog joins in. Some will become excited and others will be actively discouraged by this. Go with whatever works. Tap into what makes the breed tick...

My APBC Student colleague Graham Thompson's rescued collie "Jess" had a chase problem that he successfully turned around. He describes connecting with the core chase mechanism of a border collie like this...

"What I've found has helped is tapping into the collie eye action. Like most pure working collies, mine likes to stare at things that are static and then suddenly move. This is normal herding behaviour for her. If I wave a toy around, squeak and generally move around a lot she is not interested, but if I hold the toy in front of her and stand still, then move it suddenly, then stop for a few seconds, then move suddenly again, it really helps get her focus on it."

Once you have that focus, you can start to train your dog to retrieve the toy. How you will do that depends on how your dog is motivated. Retrieving breaks down into four distinct motor patterns, of which three are innate and one is learned. First, the chase after the toy (that's why we're here). Second the "pick-up". This is also innate and is a type of grab-bite. The "carry" is innate too and is simply the length of time your dog will hold the toy whilst moving. You've been working on enhancing the pick-up and the carry all the time you've been determining their favourite new target. Well done! The last part is the learned bit, and unsurprisingly the bit people have most trouble with. The "Leave".

There are many, many ways to teach a dog to retrieve, but with limited space I'll settle for a few examples.

The Lazy Bones:
Throw the toy and then wait until your dog brings it back. Act like you are not interested. When they nudge you with the toy, take it like it is the best gift ever and immediately throw it again. Repeat. This will only work for dogs that *really* want to retrieve.

The Grass is Always Greener:
Throw the toy and as they pick it up, immediately turn your back and play with a second, identical toy. It has to be identical because the only difference in value is the fact that they don't have this one. Kneel down and play gently with the second toy. Make it seem like you are having a brilliant game by yourself, much better than the one they are having. They will not be able to resist coming to see, and will probably drop the first toy when they get close. Immediately reward the dropping of the first toy with a throw of the second. Then pick up the first, turn your back and repeat. It will work better if you are able to throw in alternate directions, so they have to pass you with one toy in order to anticipate the next throw. This will work for almost all dogs, except those with a manic desire to hold onto their own toy.

The Gentle Touch:
First tie a curtain cord to their collar. The length will depend upon where you are working, but shouldn't need to be more than six or eight feet indoors. Throw the toy and wait until they pick it up. Silently reel them in, hand over hand with the cord. This is not a fight, just an inevitable outcome. When they arrive, gently take the toy and immediately throw it again. Repeat. If they won't release it, use the cord to get them in close then play with the second toy as above.

People get all hot and bothered through using lots of verbal encouragement. If your dog is quite happy to come to you with encouragement, and you don't mind sweating, that's fine. However, many dogs see this as a competition to keep the toy they've got, and we *never* compete with our dog. So, no, "Come here Rover" in that gruff and demanding voice whilst they stay just out of arms' reach. In fact, in these circumstances our maxim is, "least said, soonest learned". Talk gets in the way and prevents our dog learning these new rules. So, when do we tell them, "Leave"? Just as you are throwing the other ball. That's right, they've already left the first one by then, but what we're telling them is that "leave" predicts another one is coming. In future, when they hear the word "leave" they will drop what they have because they know another one is coming. The usual way of retrieve training is a bargain, "Leave that and I'll throw it again". The dog expects to lose the toy at least for a short while, in the hope that you will give it back to them. Read that again and think about it from the dog's point of view. They feel a loss when you say the word "leave". By saying "leave" as you throw the second ball, they come to expect a gain when you say the word. If you've used the word before with less than total success, use a different one such as "drop" instead, just in case it has become a signal for them to hold on tighter. Soon they'll be dropping whatever they have because "leave" predicts something better. When your dog reliably leaves on command, keep the second toy behind your back so they are unable to see that you have one. If they don't know you have, or don't have, another, you can pick up the one they've dropped and throw that one. You can shape this behaviour by insisting they drop it in a particular place, such as your hand, if you like.

Because you are still in training mode, you will be at this stage in a place without distractions (probably the living room), but now you can start to progress. Change the place first, but also make changes to the number of throws. Always finish whilst your dog is still keen, don't wait until they get fed up. Vary the distance thrown and vary the toys you use, but always keep the special one, the one you are building up to be your dog's most favourite thing in the whole world. Expect your training to regress occasionally, but keep going. If necessary return to earlier strategies to build it up again.

You now have a special toy. As in Learn to Earn, it belongs to you. Do not let them play with it alone, but bring it out for one to one games. Ask for a deferential behaviour in order to earn a throw (a sit, a down or eye contact for a few seconds) because earned rewards have more value than freebies.

Many of you may reach this stage relatively quickly, others will take weeks to get here, but regardless of the time and effort, all this is leading up to training a predictive command. "A what?" I hear you ask. A predictive command is simply a word that predicts a reliable outcome. It is classical conditioning, a word that predicts something good is going to happen. We want to train a command that reliably predicts the arrival of the special toy. It is simplicity itself. At random call the word and throw the toy to your dog. Police dog handlers use their dog's name, but most pet owners use their pet's name far too much for it to reliably predict anything. If in doubt use something brand new like "Play", "Toy" or "Ball". Say it in a pleasant quiet tone and immediately throw the toy past your dog's ear for them to chase. Do it on walks when your dog is and isn't paying attention. Make it as random as you can, that is, don't tie it to any particular behaviour. Pretty soon when you say the word they will look at you expectantly, waiting for the toy to arrive. At that point you can throw it anywhere you want, because they are watching. You can throw it to them, past them or in the opposite direction so they pass you, but always throw it, in order maintain the predictive value of the word.

Time to wave bye-bye again, this time to those owners whose dogs are now so focussed on them that they don't want to chase anything else. It's been nice working with you.

Keep up the same lifestyle for your dog and they won't need to revert to chasing again.

Right, now that the ones with the easy dogs have gone, the rest of us need to get down to some *serious* dog training.

Chapter Seven
Chase This!

Before we make a start on the best recall you can train, let's remind ourselves of where we actually are. This should be the current state of play:

- You've stopped the rot by removing your dog from the composite stimulus of their previously learned inappropriate favourite target.
- You've taken control of all the important things in our dog's life.
- You've removed as much anxiety as you can and balanced your dog's emotions.
- You've increased your obedience training and have a dog that sits ten times out of ten, and comes back when called.
- You've taken your newly introduced toy up the scale of preference of things your dog chases, but it may not be at the top yet.
- Your dog will retrieve other things if their favourite toy is not available.
- They recognise and respond to a word that communicates, "Your toy is coming".

From your dog's point of view you've:

- Increased positive interaction with you - you're fun to be with.

- Increased deference towards you - anything they want, they come through you to get it.
- Increased your value - you're really important now.
- Increased the likelihood of paying attention to you - they watch you because of the previous three.
- Increased general compliance with commands - they want to do what you say because it always has a good result.
- And reduced the likelihood of being punished - because they always get things right.

Phew! Well done so far. If you've got all that in place you're well beyond most pet dog owners and approaching the standards of the professionals. Now you're going to train the best recall ever.

Find yourself a place with as few distractions as possible. If you've got a big garden, fine, but if not go somewhere where you and your dog can concentrate. Take two toys. The first should be your dog's special toy, it should be going everywhere with you anyway. The second should be a toy that your dog will retrieve, but is not mad about. Keep the special toy in your pocket and throw the other toy a couple of times for practice.

Then sit-stay your dog and throw the lower value toy as far as you can. When it rolls to a complete halt allow your dog to chase, which is usually done by quietly saying "Fetch". As soon as your dog moves, call your predictive command and throw the special toy past their ear. The aim is for it to bounce just in front of them, to make it far more attractive than the "dead" low value toy lying further away in the grass. They will grab their favourite toy and ... it doesn't matter what happens after that. If they want to go and look for the low value toy as well, don't worry. The object was to let them know that if they are chasing something else, their special toy is still on offer. Eventually arrive at the state of affairs where you have both toys. You may have to go get the low value one yourself, but that's fine, the lesson concluded with your dog focussing on the special toy.

We now come to several ways of progressing, all of which will be dictated by your dog's response to the previous training occurrence. If your dog continues to focus on the low value toy, you can repeat exactly the same process a few times.

If your dog starts to pre-empt your predictive command and either hesitates, or doesn't go for the lower value toy, don't call or throw the special toy, but encourage them to go and pick up the low value one. Who's in charge of this training, you or them?

If they start to respond by hesitating or turning to look at you, you can leave it a bit later to use your predictive command.

You want to reach the state of affairs where your dog will run after the low value toy, but turn and look at you when you call the predictive command. What you're basically doing is introducing a low level chasing distraction for your dog. You're training them to respond to the predictive command even when they are running away from you. You probably won't hit this spot in one training session, although we did it in about twenty minutes one afternoon with one of the student's dogs at Myerscough College.

Anyway, don't rush it, there's no need. Take your time with as many training sessions as you like. Remember, short bouts and lots of them. Your aim is to have your dog stop in mid flight and look at you in expectation of the special toy, but to get there you need tiny increments. Think about the value of the first thrown toy and how it compares with the value of the special one. If you have a dog that is a manic retriever, you may have to start with a toy with very low intrinsic value and increase by varying the item. If the low value toy is moving it is more attractive to chase and if it is very close it increases in value too. Manipulate the attraction of the lower value toy in competition with the special one. What do you do if your dog does not stop for the special one? Nothing. Forget it. You made a mistake by increasing the attraction of the lower value toy beyond that of the promise of the special toy. Under no circumstances berate your dog. They did not make a mistake, you did. Water under the bridge, we learn from it and take a step back next time. If you're like me you'll inwardly curse yourself and outwardly smile, whilst planning how to get it right next time. Did I call too late? Was the lower value toy still bouncing invitingly? Should I have aimed the special toy better?

There will *always* be a point beyond which they will not recall, the "locked-on" point. Even the best trained dogs need time for the command to get from ears to brain, then brain to legs, but we're talking about the time it takes to cover less than a couple of metres here. Once your dog reaches the stage of stopping and looking back expectantly on your predictive command when they are very close to a moving lower value toy, change it for a higher value one. When you do that, compensate for the increase in intrinsic value of the new toy by allowing it to stop moving before sending your dog, and call them earlier again.

Eventually, as you keep changing them, the lower toy will be nearer and nearer in value to the special one. This may only take three toys, for example rubber ring to tennis ball to Kong, or it may take many. You will then have to use two special toys, but make sure the first one "dies" before you send your dog and that you whiz the second one past their ear accurately.

We're almost there. Progress through the same training with identical special toys. Choreograph your training like a dance. If you throw the first toy and call your dog early, they will stop on a sixpence and look at you for the second. If you call late, they will be attracted by the first toy and you may have to throw the second past their ear. Always lead by controlling your dog's response. Never become complacent. Always allow a margin of error and be prepared to throw the second toy early.

The ultimate recall is to throw the first special toy and allow your dog to chase whilst it is still bouncing then, when they are closing in on it, call your predictive command. As your dog jack-knifes round to look for the second toy you hold it aloft and give another command, "Come". Your dog will recall all the way back to you to play with the toy in your hand. Don't hesitate to show your delight.

Congratulations. You now have a dog that is fluent in recalling from one of their favourite targets for the reward of another. All we need to do now is generalise that training and we've cracked it.

Generalising means introducing distractions, so we can now practise in the park, perhaps where there are animals that are not a preferred target, or children playing, but not yet in front of the old inappropriate target or targets. Only once we've achieved fluency surrounded by distractions that are not targets can we move on.

In the same way that we've trained our dog up to now, increasing in gentle achievable increments, never allowing them to make a mistake (well perhaps not "never", because nobody's perfect, but we should aim for "never"), we're going to start to introduce the problem target.

If the problem was rabbits, we go to a field *next* to a field where rabbits *used* to live. To make sure we do not make a mistake we tie our dog out on a long line to something very sturdy, like a tree. Then we play special toy games. When we have the same brilliant recall from a moving toy as we had before, we untie the line, then we half it, and then dispense with it. Then we move into the field where rabbits *used* to live and go back to tying out. When we're perfect again we move to a field *next* to a field where rabbits live, but tied out again. Perfection there moves us into a rabbit field, but not until you've been in on your own and chased the bunnies away. Finally, on a long line for security, play your games in a field with rabbits at the other end, moving closer and closer as your dog ignores them.

I can't give you the perfect training sequence for every problem chase target, but the secret to success is in tiny attainable increments taking you closer and closer to the problem target.

The police dogs that I used to work with would run onto the training field, totally ignoring the scattering rabbits, waiting for us to catch up and throw them a Kong. The rabbits became part of the composite stimulus predicting the opportunity to chase a Kong. "If there are rabbits about it must be Kong time!"

You, too, now have the ultimate, "Chase this" command, and you will have to keep up your special toy games to maintain this level of professional control, but you can now classify yourself as a *serious* dog trainer.

I've got a little tear in my eye, not just with pride, but because almost all of you are leaving. I've thoroughly enjoyed working with you and your dogs, because it has been fun all the way. Now you're now trained to police dog standard you don't need to read any more.

However, I can understand that there will be a few of you left. Just a few, mind. You'll be the owners of the most extreme two percent of chasing dogs that have been exercising their preferences for some considerable time. The owners whose dogs *still* want to chase the rabbits, despite what we've done so far. For you, all this hard work is still going to pay off, since a solid grounding is never wasted, but we need to go even further in order to control your dogs. Remember, everything you've accomplished so far *has* worked for nearly all dogs, but we need extra measures for the most persistent of the persistent that remain.

For these dogs, it is all very well changing the target by increasing the attraction of one we can control. It will work so long as they are not allowed to reinforce previous targets by chasing them. But why should they not chase things they know are fun? They need a reason *not* to chase inappropriate targets. Which means that we need to make the problem target aversive.

Chapter Eight
Making the Problem Aversive

I don't like working with aversion. I much prefer the positive aspects of training dogs. Aversion comes with baggage attached and can have very negative effects on dogs. I do not use it lightly and I do not use it on dogs that I think it may emotionally damage. The changes implemented in the previous seven chapters will stop all but the most positive, self-assured, high drive chasing dogs from taking control of their decision about what to chase. Those we are left with are the boldest dogs that are confident in their desire to chase not only all the appropriate toys you have put in place, but also all the inappropriate targets as well. These are the dogs that will be confined to a lead for the rest of their lives, be run over in traffic, or shot for chasing livestock. Because predatory chasing is a very positive emotional state, I am prepared, having failed to control it by every other means, to reduce that positive state to a negative one in specific circumstances.

Consequently, our previous anxiety scan to check for and remove sources of ongoing stress is doubly important if we are not only going to remove a source of positive emotion, but actually change that to a negative one.

This is also why you can't just jump into the programme at this point, either. All the previous checks and balances have to be in place to ensure that you are not going to plummet your dog into misery, with all the possible additional consequences that implies.

So, what is aversion and why do we need to use it in this type of case?

When something is aversive, it is regarded as unpleasant and to be avoided. Examples of things that unconditionally stimulate aversion are pain, extreme heat or cold, loud noise and bitter tastes. "Conditioned aversion" is when a previously neutral or positive stimulus is associated with an unconditioned aversive stimulus. Aversion is always viewed from a personal perspective, for example I may be more tolerant of cold than you are, so I may not find it as aversive as you do. If all this talk of "conditioned" and "unconditioned" stimuli sounds a bit Pavlovian, it's because it is, and we need to examine Pavlov's work a little closer to understand what we are doing. Although Ivan Petrovich Pavlov won the Nobel Prize for medicine in 1904 he is probably more famous for his work on classical conditioning. In a nutshell, Pavlov demonstrated that when two things are associated together, our brain makes a connection between the two, hence when food was regularly preceded by a noise from a bell Pavlov's dogs would salivate (an uncontrollable reflex) when the bell sounded.

How does this appertain to chasing prey? When our dog chases a particular target, they make a neural connection between the pleasure of chasing and the target, so that sight, sound, smell and other parts of the composite stimulus we mentioned earlier are associated with the pleasure; that dopamine mediated endorphin buzz. This is exactly what Pavlov described as conditioning. We established that simple numbers of exposures, along with genetically determined preferences, created the priority of chase targets. This is because each time a neural connection is made it strengthens the bond. Think of it like a piece of cotton joining the "representation of a rabbit" part of the brain to the "chasing is fun" part. Neuroscientists will find this a bit over-simplified, but the gist is correct and easier to understand than long term potentiation of synaptic strength. Each time the dog performs the behaviour it adds an extra piece of cotton, a neural connection, strengthening the response. The join becomes stronger and stronger each time the dog chases a rabbit. Up until now we have concentrated on not allowing our dog to make any more joins (stopping the rot), and strengthening the join between a special toy and the "chasing is fun" part. Our aim is to have more of the latter so that the dog's preference is for the toy over the rabbit. Coupled with increased obedience and all the other measures we have put in place this will suffice for all but the most determined chasing dogs.

The reason that the most determined dogs still chase the things we'd rather they didn't is that neural connections can't be broken. I'll say that again, because it is very important. Once made, neural connections cannot be broken. The cotton threads are there forever. So, whilst we can make more connections to another target, the "rabbit" and "chase" joins will always be there.

Extinction is the process of stopping one response in favour of another. The response extinguishes when the stimulus no longer elicits it. Pavlov showed us that extinction is *not* a process of severing neural connections, but rather one of laying down new connections that eventually outweigh them.

If a bell is rung before food arrives it becomes a conditioned stimulus because it reliably predicts the primary reinforcer of food and elicits the same unconditioned response. A primary reinforcer is one that is internally reinforced. All parts of the predatory hunting sequence are primary reinforcers because the dog needs no external reinforcement for performing them. Pavlov's Bell = Food = Salivation. Therefore Bell = Salivation.

If the bell is then rung enough times without food arriving, eventually the neural connections outweigh those previously made and it predicts a lack of food, that is, Bell = No Food and fails to elicit Salivation. The Bell = Food connections still exist, but they are outnumbered by the Bell = No Food connections, which ultimately becomes the more predictable outcome, and salivation to the sound of the bell stops.

There is a problem when relating that to chasing, because the precursor to "chase" in the predatory hunting sequence is almost always "see", often after either "scent" or "track", and as the sequence is by nature sequential, early parts lead the dog to perform later ones. The dog sees the prey and goes into chase. As we know, "chase" is a primary reinforcer.

"Seeing prey", as part of the predatory hunting sequence, is also a primary reinforcer. Yes indeed, dogs get that endorphin buzz of pleasure from just seeing the things they recognise as prey!

The sight of the target also predicts the pleasure to come and stimulates the dog to perform the chase, even if they are physically unable to. Seeing the target is a conditioned stimulus to the pleasure of the chase because in the same way as Pavlov's bell, it is a reliable predictor of a primary reinforcer. Work backwards and "scenting" and "tracking" also join up.

Therefore, seeing the rabbit is both a primary reinforcer and a conditioned stimulus to the next primary reinforcer in the sequence, which is "chase". So we can't present the conditioned stimulus (the sight of the rabbit) without reinforcement and extinction can never take place as it does by ringing the bell and not offering food.

This is quite complicated, so I'll go over it again. It means we are unable to make the connection Rabbit = No Chase by presenting the conditioned stimulus (rabbit) without the primary reinforcer (chase) because each time our dog *sees* a rabbit they are reinforcing the predatory hunting sequence in relation to rabbits. We can't present the conditioned stimulus "sight of a rabbit" without the primary reinforcer "sight of a rabbit", so seeing a rabbit always elicits the chase behaviour. Therefore extinction will never take place.

We can never make sufficient connections between Rabbits = No Chase to outnumber the previous Rabbits = Chase because as long as the dog sees rabbits they will want to chase them. Unless we make a different connection: Rabbit = Unpleasant, which is why aversion is necessary. Instead of a "chase-rabbits" connection we make a new "avoid-rabbits" connection.

Where each part of the predatory hunting sequence joins the next, there is a change in motor pattern. It may happen very quickly, almost automatically, but there is a distinct change in what the dog does. To disrupt the sequence the best place to intervene is at a change point from one behaviour to the next. It is how sheepdog trialists work their dogs. The commands they give stop the dog at a change in the motor pattern: "Go left – lie down – go right – lie down – walk on – lie down." Each change is preceded by stopping the previous motor pattern before instating another. The top handlers are so good at it that it is poetry in motion. They are such good readers of their dogs and the sheep that they are able to make it look so easy, working in perfect harmony.

The other kind of sheepdog, the sheep guarders like Pyreneans and Maremmas, aren't necessarily ferocious defenders of their flock, locked in mortal combat with the wily wolf. You'd lose a lot of sheepdogs that way. Although many of the European sheep guarding breeds are large dogs, that is not the case all over the world. People as far apart as the Masai and the Navaho use smallish mongrel-looking dogs just as effectively. They work by disrupting the hunting sequence of the predator. If you are a puma stalking a sheep flock and a smallish mutt runs at you barking (a species specific defence reaction for a dog, but decidedly *not* for a sheep), it breaks the predatory sequence and you flip from hunting to defending yourself. The first avenue of defence for a wild animal is to run away from the threat, so the annoyingly woofy little dog has protected the flock without having to engage with the puma. Strangely enough, dogs don't even have to bark defensively. Just walking up to a wolf, wagging their tail, changes the wolf's mind set from hunting to social interaction, breaking the sequence just as effectively.

Remember that dogs when chasing shut down hearing and increase pain thresholds? It is very difficult to stop a dog in full flight because they are so engrossed in the action they are performing (they're about to score the winning goal in their own world cup) but we need to make the inappropriate target aversive. Therefore the best point at which to intervene is at the junction of "see" and "chase". If we make seeing the inappropriate target unpleasant it breaks the predatory sequence and no chase takes place. Inserting an aversive stimulus as the dog sees the target, but before they go into chase, conditions avoidance rather than predation. The sight of rabbits becomes a conditioned punisher not a conditioned reinforcer.

Chapter Nine
Conditioned Disgust

Having decided to use a punisher on the behaviour, we need to think about the kind of aversion we want to apply. Not all punishers are the same and some will be more appropriate than others. Punishment theory helps us put that into context. The most effective punishment is contiguous, consistent and intense enough to stop the behaviour.

Contiguous: we need the punishment to happen *at the time* the behaviour happens. We need to administer the punishment as the dog looks at the inappropriate prey target. Every second delay makes it less effective.

Consistent: we need the punishment to happen *every time* the behaviour happens. We therefore need to be in a position to apply the punisher every time our dog looks at the inappropriate prey target.

Intense: we need the punishment to be *intense enough,* from the dog's point of view, to suppress the behaviour quickly. We therefore have to find a punisher that the dog regards as being sufficiently aversive to want to stop the behaviour. Bear in mind that pain thresholds rise, incremental punishment is ineffective, and intensity will be specific to each individual. If we apply a punishment and the dog carries on chasing, all we have taught them is that they can still get that buzz, even though they are being punished. It will make chasing more, not less, likely.

You'll see from this why telling off the dog after they have come back from chasing is useless. You'll also see one of the reasons why I don't like using aversion. It is just so complicated!

Let's look at some traditional punishments for chasing sheep, a hobby that can carry the death penalty when caught in the act.

"Put the dog in a pen with a male sheep or a ewe with lambs." This is on the basis that it is just a game for the dog, but self preservation for the sheep; however there are lots of problems with this one. Firstly, we have no control over what may happen. Dog, sheep or both may be injured. There is more than one account of dogs actually killing the sheep. How resistant is the behaviour then? Regardless of the outcome, the dog may actually enjoy the battle. Even if it appears to be successful it works by making the dog frightened of sheep. That doesn't stop them barking at them in fear, which would still be considered "worrying" in legal terms.

"Use a remote controlled electric collar on the dog." Zapping the dog with an electric shock to the throat when it looks at sheep might stop it, if the shock is intense enough. Just how you measure intensity might be difficult, unless you come in at the highest pain level. In a study that used a massive electric shock to stop dogs chasing livestock, a fifth of them later barked at the sheep and goats. Regardless of its efficiency, I'm still not convinced I have the moral right to electrocute a dog.

"Introduce the dog to sheep whilst it is on a lead and tell it off for looking at them". The reason this rarely works is that it is owner dependent. When the dog is away from the owner they can choose to ignore them. It also suffers from not being intense enough. It is not enough of a punishment for the extreme chasing dogs we are dealing with. Another minus is that it is associated with the owner; the owner becomes part of the punishment. This may seriously harm the dog's bond with their owner.

"Use conditioned training discs on the dog". Conditioned properly, training discs can be a useful tool in changing dog behaviour. They signal failure of the action and the dog voluntarily stops. Unfortunately the emotions in chasing are so high that often the training discs fail to have the desired effect. They're not intense enough.

"Use a remote controlled spray collar on the dog". Whilst this has the remote benefits of the electric collar, that is the punishment is associated with the act, not the owner, again, for the most extreme dogs this may not be enough to stop the behaviour.

If any of these methods work, with the exception of the electric collar (which just has to be *extremely* painful) then the owner probably didn't need to use it because the dog wasn't sufficiently committed in the first place. Improving obedience and lifestyle would probably have had the same effect. The degree of external punishment needed is inverse to the internal reinforcement the dog receives from the behaviour. If our dog is receiving a small dopamine shot from chasing they will only need a small degree of punishment to counter it, so why use punishment when other methods will work? The bigger the dopamine shot, the less effective other methods are, and more punishment will be needed to suppress it.

The challenge is to find a punishment that doesn't hurt the dog, is intense enough to make them want to stop, isn't associated with the owner, can be monitored and applied remotely, and timed to within a second. The remote controlled citronella collar fits most of the criteria, except it isn't intense enough. But what if we could make it more intense? More aversive? What if we could make it disgusting?

Disgust is an interesting form of aversion. We all know the feeling of being disgusted. It is that hollow stomached absolute distaste that what we are experiencing is revolting. Although we relate it to different senses, we say we can see and feel things that are disgusting, it really applies to the sense of taste and evolved to keep us from eating things that are harmful.

Our sense of taste is there to protect us as well as to provide positive associations with what we eat. We, and dogs, register only five actual flavours: sweet, savoury (known as "umami"), salty, bitter and sour. Most of what we experience is actually smell, which is closely allied to taste in identifying foods. Your food isn't as tasty when you have a heavy cold, but it's actually your nose that's stifled. Whilst bitter and sour can be pleasant in tiny quantities, their main function is to prevent us from eating too much of something harmful. Many poisonous substances, rotten fruit or meat, and toxic plants have bitter or sour tastes. Registering this allows us to avoid ingesting large quantities of these substances and prevents us from at least a tummy upset, or at worst death. Consequently we avoid bitter and sour foods.

This is not a new concept when dealing with dogs. Anybody who has sprayed anti chewing liquids like "bitter apple" onto their furniture to stop puppies chewing it has used disgust as an aversive stimulus to punish their behaviour.

Taste aversion has been demonstrated in laboratory rats, wolves and people, where it has been found to have profoundly lasting effects from a single application. It makes genetic survival sense to be extra-sensitive to foodstuffs that have a bad effect on your body. Conditioning disgust isn't quite the same, but it similarly uses the mechanism of taste to create an aversive event.

The other useful property of the emotion of disgust is that, whilst painful punishers raise the heart-rate, creating more excitement and preparedness for action, disgust prompts avoidance and *decreases* the heart rate, reducing excitement. This is exactly what we want in chasing dogs.

About ninety percent of what we perceive as taste is actually smell and smell is linked to memory very robustly. If a smell reminds us of a bad taste, we will try to avoid any repeat of it. Odour memory is also very persistent, it falls off slower than other sensory memories.

We know that dogs' sense of taste is inferior to ours, but their sense of smell is vastly superior. We also know that lemon scented citronella from a spray collar has the properties of "bitter" and "sour", but not enough to be sufficiently aversive when dogs are in the state of heightened emotion associated with chasing. If we can increase the negative properties of the citronella collar to the point where dogs find it disgusting, we can associate that emotion with any inappropriate prey target to make it aversive. We need to make the taste of lemon disgusting.

This is the bad bit. The bit that if you need someone unconnected to the dog to do for you. The bit that I usually do. There are undoubtedly bad associations with me, but I don't need a good relationship with the dog like the owner does.

Take one dog, two cotton wool balls and a bottle of extra strength lemon juice.

Soak the cotton wool ball in lemon juice. Place it under the dog's top lip near to their canine tooth. Most of dogs' taste buds are towards the front of the tongue and the ones responsible for tasting "bitter" are on both sides, whilst "sour" is across the tongue slightly further back. We want to flood the taste buds with lemon juice by holding the cotton ball in place.

You will probably need to hold the dog's muzzle closed at the same time, as they will undoubtedly try to spit it out.

Adjust the amount of lemon juice on the cotton wool ball to the size of your dog. The idea is to soak their taste buds, but not actually pour any down their throat. Lemon juice can make dogs vomit and we do not want them to ingest enough to make them ill, just convince them it tastes horrid. Keep tight hold of the cotton ball, too. You don't want them to swallow that either!

People ask what to do if their dog tries to bite them whilst they are doing this. Interestingly I have never experienced it. Dogs try to squirm away and spit the cotton wool ball out, but never try to bite me. Their reaction is always one of avoidance. Disgust doesn't prompt aggression. If, by some remote possibility, you come across a dog that does react aggressively, immediately stop and return to the relationship development in chapter five.

When you have held the lemon soaked cotton ball there for thirty seconds and the dog absolutely hates the taste, remove it, soak a second ball and place that in the same position on the other side of their mouth. Remove after another thirty seconds, then leave the dog alone. Be firm in your handling, but not brutish, and don't talk. There is no need to highlight your involvement, we want the lemon to be the most relevant happening. After a lot of licking and possibly drooling for a few minutes, they will quickly recover, but they now hate the taste of lemon with total disgust. I also hate doing this, but if the option is for the dog to be confined on a lead forever, or death by motor car or for chasing livestock, I see it as the lesser of the evils.

Chapter Ten
The Final Resolution

Before we look at the final protocol, let's examine what we have done. Our dog is disgusted by the taste of lemon and will recoil at the very hint of a smell. They will also be worried by the presence of the person who administered the lemon juice, which is why you should try to get someone other than the owner to do it.

We have kept them away from the inappropriate target or targets. We still need to keep up their lifestyle changes, both the rules and the improvements. We need to keep up the obedience training and the recall and retrieve games with the predictive command for, "Chase this". It may also help if our dog wears the actual spray collar or a similar heavy collar whilst playing so that they don't learn to discriminate when the time comes to use it.

We've spent a lot of time and effort to get to this stage and we don't want to waste it all through lack of preparation now. Unless you are a very competent dog trainer, or have at least three hands, this is a two person operation. We will need the dog, the owner (or a helper if you are the owner), a remote controlled citronella spray collar, a long line that is both light and strong (I use thirty feet of parachute cord), the new favourite toy and the old inappropriate target. The helper will operate the collar so they should familiarise themselves with the operation of it away from our dog, so they aren't exposed to the smell beforehand. Discuss the exact course of action that will follow so you both know precisely how to respond. Things will happen very quickly and we don't want to mistime our best opportunities. If you think you need to, you can do a dry run without the dog to establish what will happen in each eventuality, for example if *that* happens then we will do *this*, if *the other* happens we will do *this*. Once ready, we take the dog to the appointed place. Before we get there we need to secure the spray collar on the dog and attach the long line to their ordinary collar. This should be a strong comfortable neck collar, or a body harness, *not* a head collar. If you drive there, attach the line and the collar as the dog gets out of the car. If you are walking, try to do it at least fifty yards, or a few minutes, before you get to the place. Do *not* test the spray collar anywhere near the dog. There is no need to speak to the dog, just go for a walk. The long line should be loose to simulate freedom, but hold tightly on to the end for absolute safety. You are aiming to come upon the problem target as though it just happened at random. If you can't reliably find the target, make a recognisance visit first and come back prepared. This training exercise should be set up to succeed.

When our dog "accidentally" comes across the old target there will be a split second when they first see it, but before they start to chase. At that point press the maximum dose of spray. Spray the dog for seeing the target. As they recoil, the owner should call the predictive command and run in the opposite direction waving the toy. When the dog's attention is on their owner, they should throw the toy and have an exciting play session, away from the problem target. Play for as long as the dog is up for it, then stop and allow them to get their breath back.

What could go wrong? The worst that can happen is that we mistime our spray. Too early and we've randomly punished something else. It'll make the subsequent punishment of looking at the target a bit less effective, but it's not the end of the world. Too late and the dog sets off in hot pursuit. Try one spray, on the slight chance that it will work. It usually doesn't for the reasons we have already discussed. Don't keep pressing the spray because you'll teach the dog they can work through the disgust. Try to stop them as gently as you can with the line, reel them in and put them back on the lead. Don't speak, abandon the exercise, go to a different place and try again from scratch. Don't berate the dog. It isn't their fault. We made a mistake. Pack up the gear, move on and try again later.

We might be worried about the citronella scent hanging around in our dog's ruff after we have used it, continuing the aversive association, but this is less of a problem than you might think. Adaptation to an aversive smell is quite quick. The intensity of the smell reduces by half within one second and we lose the ability to smell it completely within one minute. Increases in the intensity of an aversive smell however, are immediately re-registered. As a police officer I occasionally had the unpleasant duty of entering houses where people had been dead for some time. The smell as I entered the house was almost unbearable, but sensory adaptation meant that within a minute I didn't notice it anymore. Unfortunately, if I had to go out and come back in again I was back to square one. Young police officers quickly learn that it is best to wait for the undertaker with the body, rather than go out and have to return inside again. Our dog won't register an increase in intensity until we press the spray again.

And presuming we got it right, we go again. Walk back in the direction of the inappropriate prey target and try to come upon it again. It is possible that this time our dog will be apprehensive about what is happening, but we need to condition the sight of the problem target to the spray. Once could be a coincidence, but twice sets up our conditioning. The dog will be probably be more reluctant to chase and may even be reluctant to look at the old problem target, but carry on with it nevertheless. When the dog looks at the old target, press, spray, predictive command and play. If they simply refuse to look, abandon this occasion and move on to the next. Twice will be enough before we move location anyway. Now we stop this discrete exercise and set up another one. The format is exactly the same, but we want to condition the old target in a different place, so we are conditioning only the target, not the place. To do that we need to separate the next episode in time and space from the last one. The easiest way I've found to do this is to pop the dog into the car and go for a short drive to another place. If you have to walk, make sure you don't come across any other problem targets on the way.

When you arrive at the next place, repeat the conditioning process of "look, press, spray, predictive command and play" twice more. The dog should now be showing some apprehension when they see the target and it's time to pack up for the day.

There *are* variables. Some dogs will only need one spray in a single place to avoid the old target from then on. Some may need two sprays in three or four different locations before they understand the conditioning is to the target and no other stimulus in the environment.

The next day take the dog to the original place, on the long line and wearing the spray collar. When they first see the inappropriate prey, the owner should call the predictive command and play with the favourite toy. The dog will avoid the inappropriate, now disgusting, target in favour of their favourite toy. If they don't do so immediately, go back to the "spray, predictive command and play". You can proof this in as many places as you like now, but you shouldn't need to spray. If your dog has multiple targets each one will have to be conditioned using the above method, so you will need to "look, press, spray, predictive command and play" each one.

As the owner continues to use the predictive command and play every time the dog looks at inappropriate prey, eventually the dog will look at old prey and come to their owner to play instead. There is just a chance that our dog will seem fine for a while, but just once, usually when we have been lulled into a false sense of security, revert to the old target. We need to make sure that the owner is aware of this possibility and that they should monitor their dog's behaviour closely. This is not a breakdown of the training. It is a recognised consequence of changing behaviour, known as spontaneous recovery of the previous behaviour. Remember, the neural connections are still there, we've just laid down some new ones to compete with them. For this reason our dog should continue to wear the collar for about a week afterwards, but usually it isn't needed.

What have we done? We've kept punishment to an absolute minimum. We've caused no pain nor risked physical injury. We've made the problem target, be it sheep, rabbits, joggers or cars, disgusting. There is no signal for, "Don't do that!", only a positive one for "Do this!" The owner only ever provides their dog with praise and pleasant effects. The dog avoids the conditioned disgusting stimulus and prefers to interact with their owner instead.

So, is our dog cured? Only in as much as they now find the target or targets that we have conditioned to be disgusting and will no longer be interested in them. They still have the desire, the need, for that fix of chasing, so all the positive aspects of the behaviour modification programme stay in place.

But how tough can it be, playing retrieve games with your dog, having the ultimate reward for your dog in your hand, being the focus of your dog's attention, the apple of their eye? Stopping predatory chasing isn't about trying to forbid your dog from enjoying themselves whilst you pull out your hair in despair. It is about forging a deep understanding between you, where you are the best thing in your dog's life and they provide you with endless enjoyment.

Predatory chase dogs can seem difficult to control, but as well as making the best police dogs there are, they can also be the most rewarding pets, once you get inside their heads.

Appendix
The APBC

The Association of Pet Behaviour Counsellors (APBC) is an international network of experienced and qualified pet behaviour counsellors, who, on referral from veterinary surgeons, treat behaviour problems in dogs and other pets.

Please note that members are usually unable to answer questions about individual cases by e-mail or give telephone advice because of the need to establish an accurate diagnosis, determine motivation and discuss the appropriate treatment programme in detail.

You can find your nearest APBC member through www.apbc.org.uk or by contacting the general office at PO Box 46, Worcester, WR8 9YS, England. Telephone 01386 751151. Email: info@apbc.org.uk

Website

You can find further information about David Ryan from his website at www.dog-secrets.co.uk

Printed in Great Britain
by Amazon